DEC 2008

Kanner Architects

11 Projects

ORO *editions:*
Publishers of Architecture, Art, and Design
Gordon Goff & Oscar Riera Ojeda – Publishers
West Coast: PO Box 150338, San Rafael, CA 94915
East Coast: 143 South Second Street, Suite 208, Philadelphia, PA 19106
www.oroeditions.com
info@oroeditions.com

Kanner Architects
1558 10th Street, Santa Monica, CA 90401
www.kannerarch.com

Editor: Christopher Keough
Book Design: Studio Morris
Additional Design: Lincoln Tobier, Alexander Simpson

All photography: John Edward Linden, except;
Pages 24-29: PUMA International, PUMA North America
Cover and pages 66-67, 70-75: Benny Chan
Pages 8 and 80: D. Ingres
Computer renderings: Kanner Architects, Krai Charuwatsuntorn

Printed in China by ORO *editions* HK

ISBN 0-97746-723-6

Distribution:

In USA	Europe	Asia
Distributed Art Publishers, Inc.	Art Books International	Page One
155 Sixth Avenue, Second Floor	The Blackfriars Foundry, Unit 200	20 Kaki Bukit View
New York, NY	156 Blackfriars Road, London	Kaki Bukit TechparkII
10013	SEI 8EN	Singapore 415967

Kanner Architects

11 Projects

Introduction by Michael Webb

Thoughtful Simplicity

Michael Webb

The house that Stephen Kanner built for his family in Pacific Palisades exemplifies the qualities his talented firm brings to all its varied projects. It turns an irregular, confined lot to advantage by stepping down a hillside and opening up to a sunny, verdant garden. Inventive use is made of inexpensive materials, from the combed plaster of the exterior to the concrete floors, fiberboard, and plywood cabinetry within. The interiors are airy and full of natural light, and every space leads you forward to another intriguing vista. Above all, the house is joyful and free-spirited, as welcoming to visitors as it is a cozy fit for the couple and their two little daughters.

Kanner Architects creates rational, humane, and inspiring environments. All are tailored to their sites and to the clients' needs and budget. Frugal or expansive houses, elegant and low-income apartments, an international chain of PUMA flagship stores, an exuberant gas station, and a high-rise residential tower: each of the projects included in this survey of recent work has its own distinct personality. They are also members of an extended family that share the traits of rigor, openness, and springiness, combined with a strong sense of place. Though the firm is now building far beyond its home base in Santa Monica, most of its projects are still located in Southern California and are infused with the buoyant spirit and legacy of that region.

Growing up in Los Angeles, not far from where he lives now, Kanner understood from an early age how a building should respond to light, a benign climate, and the beauties of nature. As the son and grandson of architects, his career was practically ordained, and he joined the family firm in 1983, soon after graduating from University of California, Berkeley with a masters degree in architecture. It was a respected practice, noted for its pragmatism and craft. His father was part of the postwar Case Study House generation, which took the precepts of modernism as a given; Stephen found himself drawn to the populist tradition of vibrant billboards, Googie coffee houses and Disney's Tomorrowland. Charles Kanner had explored the world of pop in his paintings; Stephen created his own ironic, inventive version of strip architecture. The In-N-Out drive-thru in Westwood Village is the culmination of that brief but fertile phase, which won the firm a lot of publicity.

The house was originally designed in the same vein—an angled pink stucco block, studded with portholes—but friend and colleague Joe Addo urged him to exercise restraint. As built, the house is full of playful details; it marks the end of one form of expression and the start of something new. Kanner, who succeeded his father as principal in 1998, is still partial to free forms and bright hues, but he employs them sparingly and only as the project demands.

The ambitious owner of an independent gas station on a heavily trafficked intersection of Los Angeles wanted a unique attraction, and Kanner Architects responded with a daringly cantilevered canopy inspired by the coiled ramps of a freeway intersection, and a steeply inclined driveway wrapped around a cylindrical glass tower. A 60-unit block of low income apartments at Hollywood and Western takes a cue from the tiled mosaic on service structures that emerge from the subway station below. Colored squares turn the gridded façade

Michael Webb is the author of twenty books on architecture and design, most recently Art/Invention/House and Adventurous Wine Architecture, and is a contributing writer for Architectural Digest, The Architectural Review, and Frame.

of three staggered bays into a Mondrian canvas, reducing the bulk and distracting attention from the bare-bones detailing. Malibu 5, a house in the hills above the coast highway, employs terra cotta red for all its walls and flat roofs. Kanner found the color on a rural museum in Africa, where he is collaborating with Addo on a block of condominiums in the Ghanaian capital of Accra. He justified the bright hue by reference to the wildflowers that grow on the site.

These dynamic forms and colorful surfaces are photogenic, but the importance of the firm's work lies in its fusion of structure and volume. Boldly modeled boxes are raised on recessed bases so that they appear to float above the ground. Planes wrap around expansive windows to impart drama and depth, and to screen or diffuse sunlight. There is a harmony of proportion and an easy flow of space. At every point, you are aware of the building as a whole, its felicitous placement on the site, and the way each part builds anticipation for the next. Following his brief detour into popular imagery, Kanner has returned to the modernist fold, creating buildings that are crisp and cool, yet full of soul.

There's a constant search for unique ways to design conventional buildings and create uplifting spaces with a lightness of touch. The two volumes of Malibu 5 are rotated to command views of hillside and ocean and are pulled apart to bring natural light to the center of the house. The linear Malibu 3 house, which replaces one destroyed by wildfire in a Malibu canyon, offers two-way views and cross-ventilation for every room. There are echoes of De Stijl and R.M. Schindler in the asymmetrical geometries, though Kanner has developed his own distinctive language, which uses these pioneers as a point of departure. His warm Modernism is about problem solving, not ideology, and it has the timeless appeal of architecture that's driven by content rather than style.

All projects start with intensive research and detailed discussions with the client. "There's a spontaneity in the process of looking at the site, feeling the breeze, considering the context, materials, and sustainability," says Kanner. "I may be thinking of thirty things at once before an idea emerges. Sketching is an essential part of the process—I grew up at a time when architects still knew how to draw and even now, in the computer age, the human brain and hand are the best tools."

Every job is a collective endeavor. Early on, Kanner involves one or more of his five design associates to develop the ideas three dimensionally. Other members of the 30-person firm work out the details to achieve a fresh and creative solution. For a nightclub, younger staff members provided personal expertise to shape the design. The goal is always to find the most appropriate form of expression, satisfying practical needs while making people feel good, and doing this as simply and efficiently as possible.

Kanner has led a flourishing practice while serving as president of the AIA/LA Chapter, founding the A+D Museum of Los Angeles, and developing mentoring programs for architectural students. Many of the firm's buildings have won awards, and these have brought the firm commissions to design large-scale commercial and institutional projects, alongside the houses it does so well.

United Oil Gasoline Station
Los Angeles, California

*Previous spread: United Oil
gas station is inspired by
the sculptural qualities
of the ubiquitous freeway
interchanges that dot the
Southern California landscape*

*Below: a preliminary study
of form, developing the inter-
change analogy and circulation
patterns at project site*

*Opposite: 3-D study model
of site at La Brea and
Slauson avenues*

Interpreting an everyday structure that's taken for granted, Kanner designed a service station inspired by the car culture in which he grew up. The United Oil Gasoline Station delivers a union of a city's historic love affair with the automobile and the contemporary one-stop shop of immediate gratification and convenience.

Drawing inspiration from freeway interchanges, the design employs two soaring planes. One, made of concrete, delivers customers up and over the store and back down into a carwash. The other, a curvilinear metal form is the roof of the retail space and extends in an upward trajectory to the front of the site where it ends as a 30-foot canopy over the pumps.

Inside the store, which is screened with a curving glass wall, the service counter is encased in a 28-foot glass tower that mimics the steel containers of the nearby oil field. An existing billboard on the site contributes to the project's roadside marker image. The station engages the billboard by trying to compete for motorist attention.

Park Tower

Los Angeles, California

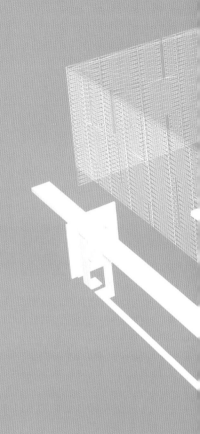

Previous spread: rendering of Park Tower in Downtown context at twilight

This spread: a study of how the building addresses the street at Ninth and Hope

Following spread: by integrating a rendering with a comprehensive picture of Downtown Los Angeles, the building's unique architectural elements emerge

Park Tower's multidimensional form and design are a response to the building's urban context. It is designed to be all things to all interests: a proud addition to the Downtown skyline, a comfortably livable residential tower and a respectful neighbor.

To achieve this lofty goal, the building comprises distinct vertical components. At its base are two stories of retail space, double-height with high ceilings and mezzanines. At Ninth and Hope streets, the street-level corner is a framed glass cube that relates to the pedestrian scale of the street with its wide sidewalks, trees, lighting and furniture.

Moving upward, an eight-story pedestal relates to the mid-rise scale of the neighboring projects. Complementing this is the building's parking garage, situated to the north, which is topped with a swimming pool and gardens.

The volume above the pedestal corresponds to the scale of a Downtown skyline. Thin, richly articulated faces on the north and south combine with longer, crystalline planes on the east and west. These veil-like, green-tinted curtain walls are animated by rhythmically placed cut-outs, protrusions and landscaped terraces. These articulations, and the use of varied materials and the minimal use of mullions distinguish this tower as a place to live and not a corporate office building.

To open views into Grand Hope Park across Ninth Street, the south façade is articulated with a rhythm of balconies and shielded from direct sun by a corseted brise soleil.

A large setback four levels from the building's top establishes still another piece of its vertical composition. The terrace, lushly landscaped with trees, provides generous outdoor space for three levels of penthouse units.

For the top of the project, ribbons of glass extend from the east and west curtain walls and loop over the upper-most floor, forming a translucent roof that will be illuminated at night and sparkle in daytime sunshine. Mechanical systems are recessed below this summit.

Inside, the building's two-, three- and four-bedroom units will have full-height windows and large balconies. Environmentally sensitive features include photovoltaic arrays, recycled building materials, passive heating and cooling systems that include the brise soleil and operable windows.

Ross Snyder Gymnasium
Los Angeles, California

The 12,000-sf Ross Snyder Recreation Center is a mosaic of cubic forms that, through color and varied size and materials, abstractly represent the diversity of the South Los Angeles community in which the center was built.

The campus's different forms house a gym, several community rooms, offices, a kitchen and restrooms. Concrete block walls have insulative properties and the balance of the materials—metal panels, tiles, stainless steel, glass block and metal siding—make a building that will endure and require very little maintenance year to year.

Strategically placed windows minimize direct sunlight, easing cooling requirements, while skylights and clerestory windows permit ample natural light. The gymnasium is the centerpiece of a park that is integral to the social livelihood of the community.

Opposite: northeast corner,
materials correspond to the
interior program

Below: south elevation;
white box on left is a
classroom, larger form on
right is the gymnasium

PUMA *International*

Left to right: preservation and
integration of façade, Antwerp

Cash wrap, Antwerp

Merchandise story, Antwerp

Shoe wall, Antwerp

Mirror wall across from fitting
rooms, Antwerp

Left to right: fitting rooms,
Cologne
Fitting rooms, Antwerp
Shoe wall, PUMA red wall,
looking to street, Philadelphia
Pennsylvania

PUMA International became something of a design lab for Kanner Architects. Much of the architectural language found in the firm's buildings can be traced to some degree to the forms and vocabulary of interior design that appears in PUMA stores in Asia, Europe and North America.

While developing the red-and-white PUMA store concept, Kanner worked closely with British design and advertising agency GBH to fashion a mirthful shopping experience that incorporates high-tech innovation (a holographic roaming PUMA, interactive merchandise displays) and graphic escapes (incongruously themed fitting rooms) with the retailer's ultra-styled products.

The architectural forms, or kit of parts, developed for PUMA, include a series of folding and shifting planes, designed as abstractions of the brand's leaping cat logo. Working exclusively in existing buildings, many of which are historic, the designs use double height ceilings, lofts, mirrors and articulated walls to open spaces and suggest consumer traffic patterns. Color, as in a red rear wall with the PUMA logo, compels visitors to circulate among display systems laid out as merchandising stories. Independent product lines narrate the story of a global urban brand.

The aesthetic remains minimal, propping up the merchandise as the clear focus of attention.

Metro Hollywood
Los Angeles, California

Metro Hollywood Transit Village is both a social statement and an exercise in contemporary design. Kanner Architects approached the building with the idea that high-density, transit-oriented development can be achieved within reasonable budgets and with architecturally interesting design.

Metro Hollywood puts people in affordable residences that they can be proud to call home and that are near to jobs and/or transportation to jobs and amenities. Because of its scale and prominent location at a visible and highly trafficked intersection, the structure had to make a statement about urban living.

The mixed-use 60-unit, low-income housing project contains mostly two- and three-bedroom apartments over 10,000 sf at ground level that includes retail space and a child care center. The project exceeds by 20 percent state codes regarding energy efficiency.

The design integrates the building with the neighborhood by lining up its large courtyard with the existing courtyard of the project's prior phase. In addition to being cost-effective, it has a colorful, uplifting contemporary design that is aesthetically compatible with the design features of the existing Metro rail station below.

Heavy steel frames to support the project above the subway station were costly and required creative solutions to maintain budget. Kanner used colorfast painted plaster rather than more expensive materials to mimic the color pallet of the MTA station. Windows were arranged strategically to provide views for residents and break up what otherwise could have been an impenetrable façade.

Below: a typical corner unit with generous views and natural light

Courtyard provides a splash of green in a dense urban neighborhood and provides a common space for residents

Opposite: approach from street on west elevation along Western Avenue

Bentley-Massachusetts
Los Angeles, California

The Bentley-Massachusetts Apartments in Los Angeles's Westwood neighborhood was designed to recall a pioneer of mid-century Modernism.

Calling on Richard Neutra's Landfair, Kelton and Strathmore apartment buildings, the four-story building (with spacious penthouses on the top floor) achieves a dual objective per its Southern California setting. The location and density provide residents with the opportunity to live the urban lifestyle of Los Angeles while walls of glass, balconies and top-floor terraces allow access to the sunlight and coastal breezes.

This dual persona continues when considering the structure's presence at day and night. During daylight hours the building is horizontal and streamlined. When the sun sets, the effect is quite different. The building takes on a romantic lantern-like presence. The figure/ground relationship of the plaster and glass reverses and warm light finds its way to the street below.

The cantilevered second floor lifts the building off the ground and sets it back from the street, creating a sense of lightness and giving the impression the building is floating.

Below: outdoor balcony
along building façade

Opposite: northeast corner
along Bentley Avenue

511 House

Los Angeles, California

Previous spread: view from
street showing main entrance
between garage and stair tower

Below: second floor sunlit
corridor

Opposite: twilight view of
house with double-height
living room in foreground

511 House, a 3,500-sf two-story home, is designed to take full advantage of the
bright light and cool Southern California breezes of Los Angeles's Pacific Palisades
neighborhood. The top design objective was to create a living space with little
differentiation between inside and outside. The glass-clad main body was pushed
to the north side of a lot the size of a tennis court (60 feet by 120 feet). A wide patio
used extensively for dining and play extends to the south of the lower level. Large
sliding glass doors can disappear—along with the distinction between inside and
outside—and provide a conduit for soothing sea breezes.

The modernist aesthetic of 511 House draws inspiration from nearby houses created
by Richard Neutra and Charles and Ray Eames. At the same time, it is of its time and
unique as its textures, materials and windows make a personal statement. There is a
metaphorical juxtaposition of rough to smooth materials (scratch-coat plaster versus
smooth mosaic tile) that recalls the relationship of the ocean to the mountains.

Landscaping was the key to privacy. The property was screened with timber bamboo,
black bamboo and ficus hedges in front of horizontally slatted cedar-fencing. At the
street a "V" shaped specimen palm layers the front façade while bands of Japanese
grass, gravel and lawn graphically recall the scoring pattern in the front yard hardscape.

The 511 House is about Southern California living. The plan, section and site plan are of
greatest importance. How can a typical lot be utilized to make it seem larger and more
open? Solving the planning problems in a unique way allows the design of the envelope
to become secondary.

Below and opposite: walls of glass allow for natural light to fill interior volumes and provide a seamless transition to the garden

Contrary to the desire of many clients who want their home to blend with its surroundings, the owner of Malibu 3 asked for something that would stand out of context, defiant toward the very setting and conditions that led to a fire that claimed his original home on the same site.

The solution was to design an expression of resilience. As it must stand against immense weather conditions, fires, winds, floods, Malibu 3 is designed to observe and view nature and never again be consumed by it. The exterior, with its white porcelain tiles, also refers to the client's professional identity as a dentist.

The design must have been effective: the client chose the name Simpatica Sem, a mix of Italian and Tibetan, which intimates the spiritual blending of mind and soul.

Two cubes linked by a glazed corridor, the house's simplicity counters the complexity and wildness of the rugged hills that surround it. The structure's extruded composition is a reaction to many conditions of the project: the site's linear topography; a desire for massive window openings to take in spectacular views of mountains immediately outside and the ocean in the distance; and the need for fire resistance.

The home is set into a cutout on a hill, with a concrete retaining wall on one side and walls of glass eager to receive the sun on the other. The second story of this single-loaded building has vistas of both the mountains and canyons with their dramatic weather changes and the ocean beyond.

A mere 25 feet wide, the building's lean profile provides excellent cross-ventilation of abundant sea breezes. The layered composition of the west elevation allows for large dual-glazed openings with numerous projections designed to shade the glass. The design worked so effectively that it met California Energy Standards without tinting the glass.

The home's interior is a mixture of cool and warm. The main level, with its common spaces, has a floor of concrete pavers. The bedrooms upstairs are carpeted. The presence of marble (white, blue and matte-black) and cherry on both levels tie together the whole.

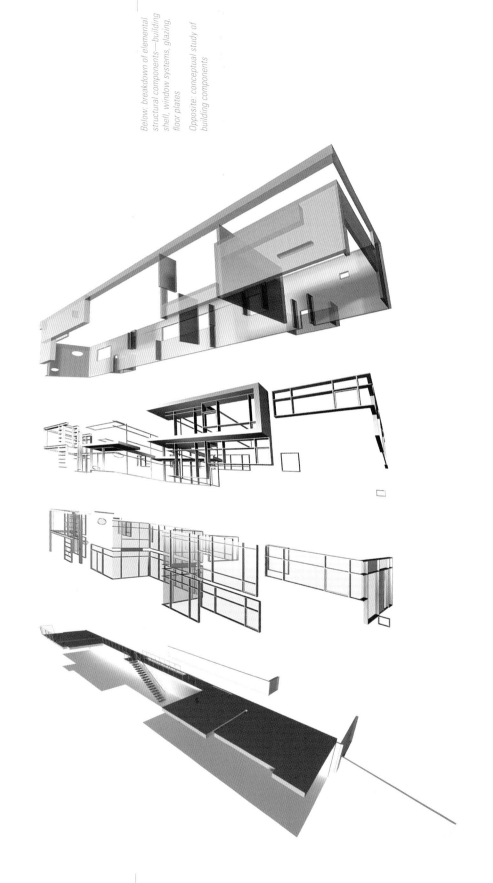

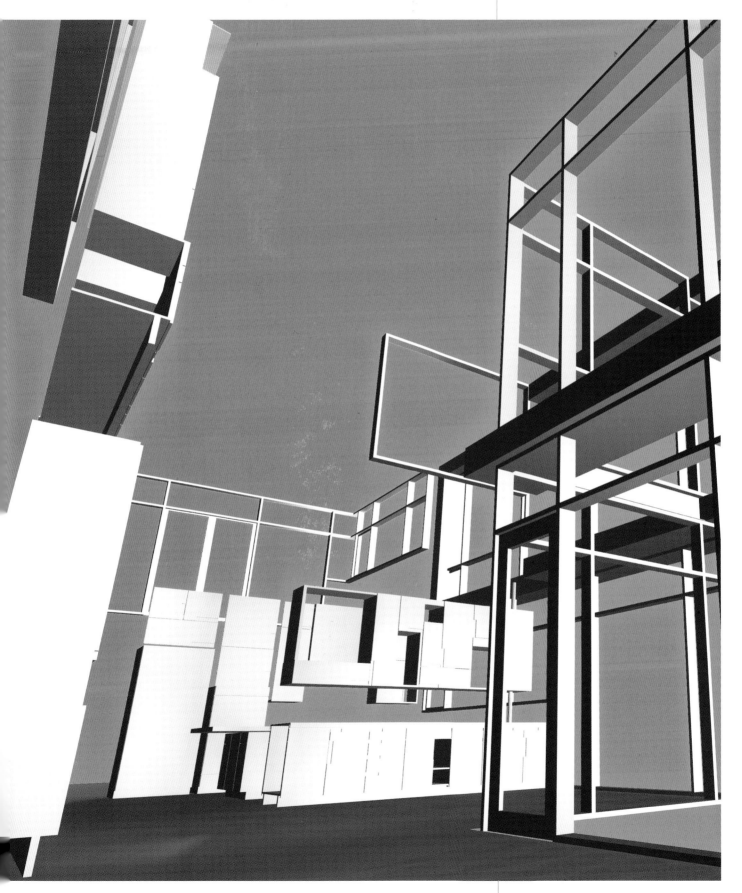

Previous spread: multi-faceted cedar-clad building serves double purpose as home office and guesthouse

Below left: view into office entrance

Below right: interior view of waiting area

Opposite: southwest corner, waiting room/guesthouse bedroom

Tucked neatly on a lush hillside behind a home, Canyon View is an exercise in camouflage and dual purpose. Riffing on the organic qualities of its surroundings and the treehouse next door, the designers fashioned an office for the psychologist who lives in the main home. The angled cedar wall planes break the structure into a series of small spaces that help it blend into the landscape and converse with the eucalyptus trees in their midst.

With its vertical grain Douglas fir-beamed ceilings and built-ins of the same material, this comfortable and disarming place for clients also serves the psychologist by eliminating the debilitating Los Angeles commute. Although mere paces from her proper home, it is nonetheless a completely different experience and therefore a de facto sanctuary from the distractions of daily life.

The waiting room and office/consultation area have separate entrances and can double as bedroom and living area when the office fulfills its second purpose: guesthouse. Canyon View has a bathroom and hallway kitchenette to accommodate short-term stays.

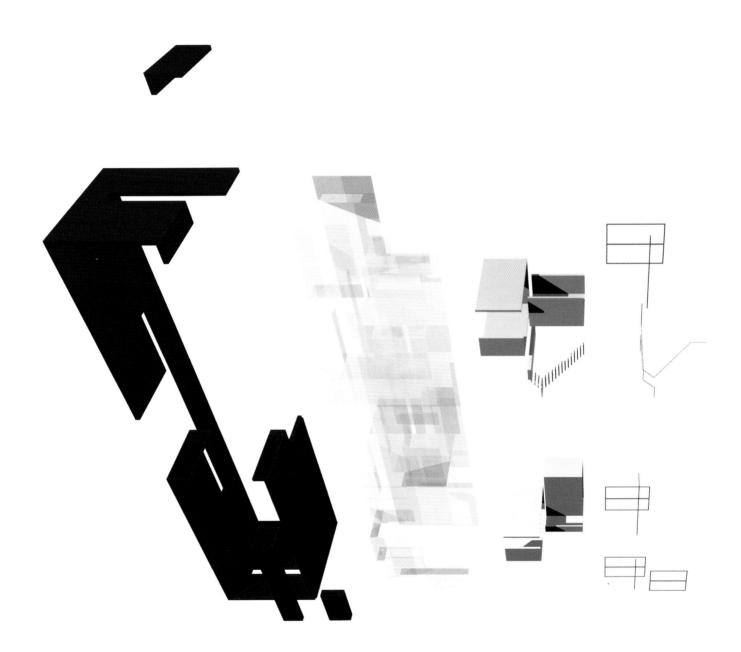

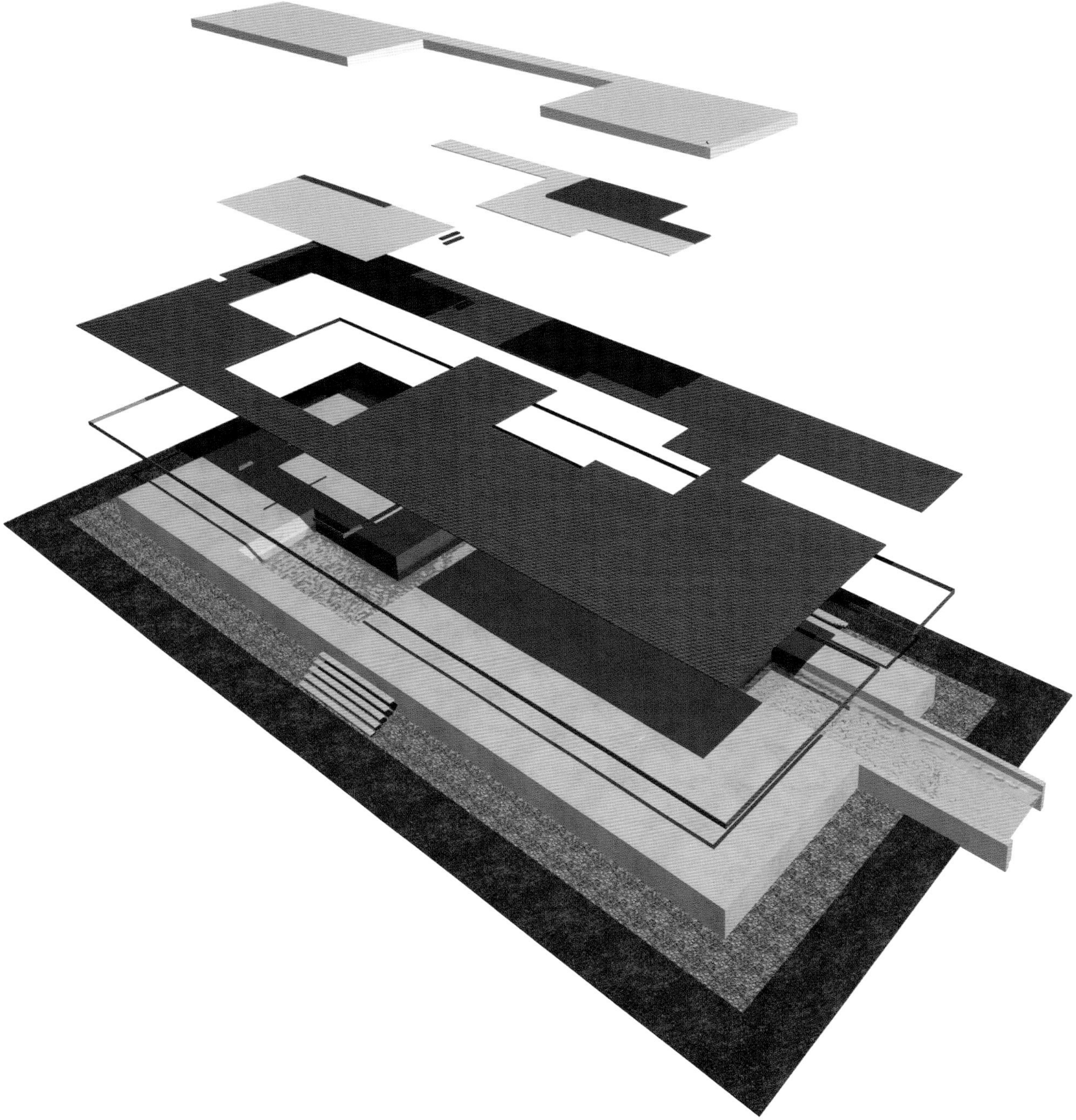

Previous spread: Lot 30's interior spaces, wrapped in a red cedar container agrow in the woods at night

This spread: exploded diagram of building's components

Sagaponac Lot 30 is one of 34 homes commissioned by New York developer Coco Brown to occupy a unique subdivision in the Hamptons in New York. Brown's development of contemporary homes was conceived as a foil to the proliferation of mansions elsewhere in the Hamptons. Kanner's contribution is a weekend home designed to make the most of its heavily wooded setting.

Because the house is shielded by trees, it can be clad in glass without compromising privacy. The two narrow glass volumes are wrapped in cedar and raised on a plinth to reach high into the tree canopy for light.

The cedar skin, stained to symbolize the colors of autumn in the Northeast, is broken in parts and pieces are placed on axes away from the house. These extruded pieces continue the inside/outside rhythm of the building itself, tying the site to the structure and bringing the site into the home at the same time it puts the living space outside.

Opposite: living room interior
and glass stairway

Below: glass façade puts
residents in nature, open
horizontal form allows cross-
ventilation and views from
all rooms

Malibu 5

Malibu, California

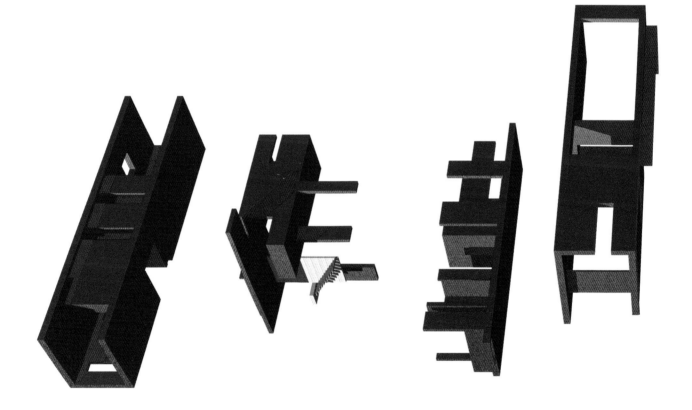

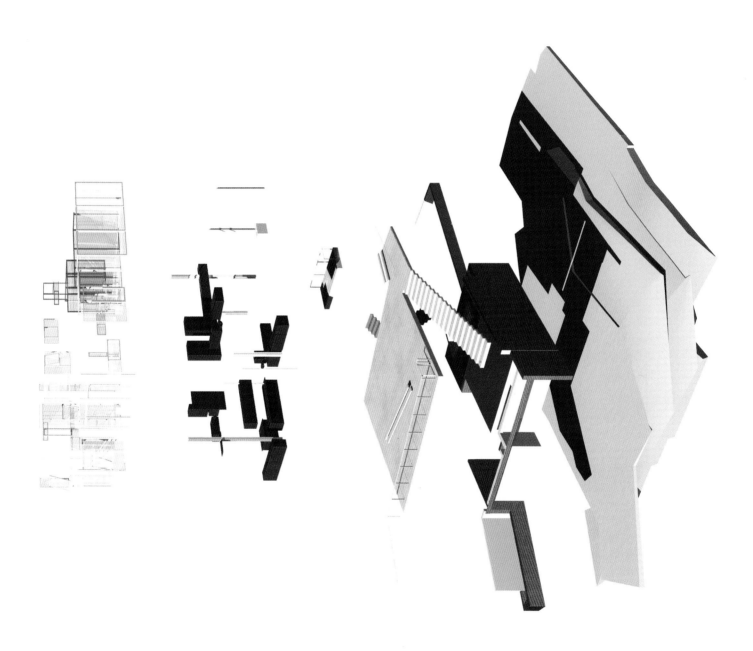

Vertically stacked in asymmetry and set into a Malibu hillside above the vast Pacific Ocean, Malibu 5 is an ecofriendly Modernist home. Among the energy-efficient systems that make minimal use of the power grid are ground-level concrete floors that act as heat sinks and provide radiant heating. Energy capturing solar panels contribute power to the local utility during daylight hours. Other green aspects of the home are the use of recycled building materials and solar water panels that heat water for domestic uses.

Two lean C-shaped rectangular bars—one is two stories tall, the other is a single story over the garage—are split by a linear courtyard. This separation creates space for the ocean breezes to penetrate the structure and perform passive cooling.

The two halves of the house are cantilevered and give it a floating quality. All rooms open on two sides to facilitate cross ventilation. The home faces the Pacific Ocean to take advantage of coastal breezes, energy-providing solar gain and natural light. Its landscaping mimics the surrounding sloped, rocky hillside. Rocks from the site are recycled in the landscape and their red color inspired the selection of paint for the scratched plaster exterior. The color reminded Kanner of an earth tone he discovered while visiting West Africa.

*Opposite: view through
living room to Pacific Ocean
Below: glass-enclosed
living room*

MAGAZINES

INTERIORS, August 2006, South Korea – Kanner Architects Studio

Architecture, July 2006 – Roadside Attraction – United Oil Gasoline Station

Architectural Record, July 2006 – Residential News – Metro Hollywood Transit Village

INTERNI & Décor, July 2006, South Korea – Environmentally Sensitive Buildings in Modern Design – profile of Stephen Kanner including 511 House, Pacific Palisades Gymnasium, Malibu 3

MFL (Magazine For Living), July 2006, Italy – Malibu House – Malibu 3

Los Angeles Business Journal, June 12, 2006 – Going Ghana – Q&A with Stephen Kanner

Robb Report Vacation Homes, April/May 2006 – Phoenix Rising – Malibu 4

Hise, April 2006, Slovenia – Canyon View Office/Guesthouse, 511 House

Szép Hézak, April 2006, Hungary – 511 House

Trends, Spring 2006 – Point of difference – Canyon View Office/ Guesthouse

INTERIOR DESIGN, March 2006 – twice as nice – Malibu 4

INTERIOR DESIGN, January 2006 – crosslines: good genes – profile of Stephen Kanner

INTERIORS, January 2006, South Korea – PUMA Chicago

COMPETITIONS, Winter 2005/2006 – Satellite Offices as Community Destination - Pacoima Neighborhood City Hall

Trends, December 2005 – Natural Exhibition – Malibu 4

Architectural Digest, November 2005 – Unbuilt Houses: Modernism in Context – Rambla Pacifico

INTERIORS, November 2005, South Korea – Malibu 3

KAZA, 2005, Brazil – Benedict Canyon House

Los Angeles Times Magazine, October 30, 2005 – A Space Apart – Canyon View Office/Guesthouse

Umran, September 2005, Saudi Arabia – 511 House

Architecture, July 2005 – The Transit Village Timetable – Metro Hollywood Transit Village

Villák, Summer 2005, Hungary – Malibu 3

Interior Digest, February 2005, Russia – Malibu 3

Interior Design, Intervention: Hollywood Ending – Metro Hollywood Transit Village

Wired, October 2003 – The Architecture Zoo – Sagaponac Lot 30

Wohn! Design, May/June 2003, Germany – Number 511 – 511 House

Vanity Fair, May 2003 – 37 Ways of Looking at a Hampton – Sagaponac Lot 30

Haute, March 2003, Korea – Kanner Residence – 511 House

Los Angeles Times Magazine, December 8, 2002 – Setting Sail: An architect creates a nautically inspired house in Pacific Palisades – 511 House

l'Arca, June 2002, Italy – Houses of Sagaponac – Sagaponac Lot 30

Architectural Record, May 2002 – American Institute of Architects Honor Awards – In-N-Out Burger

Metropolis, May 2002 – Inside the Box: Stephen Kanner reveals his Modernist lineage in a new family home – 511 House

Dwell, April 2002 – Here Come the Neighborhoods – Sagaponac Lot 30

GQ, October 2001 – News Flash – PUMA

Blueprint, May 2001, England – A Woodland Invasion of High Society – Sagaponac Lot 30

Architectural Record, April 2001 – Record News: 34 top architects selected for Hamptons houses – Sagaponac Lot 30

Abitare, May 2000, Italy – The Architecture of California – overview of Kanner Architects current work

BOOKS

LA 2000+: New Architecture in Los Angeles, John Leighton Chase (The Monacelli Press 2006)

Beach Houses, Casey Mathewson (Feierabend, 2006)

Out of Town, Peter Hyatt (Images Publishing, 2006)

Today's Country Houses, Jacobo Krauel (Carles Broto i Commena, 2005)

Architecture Now! 3, Philip Jodidio (Taschen, 2004)

The Inspired Retail Space, Corinna Dean (Rockport Publishers, 2003)

American Dream – The Houses at Sagaponac: Modern Living in the Hamptons, Coco Brown, Richard Meier and Alastair Gordon (Rizzoli International Publications, 2003)

Another 100 of the World's Best Houses, (Images Publishing, 2003)

Brave New Houses: Adventures in Southern California Living, Michael Webb (Rizzoli International Publications, 2003)

100 of the World's Best Houses, (Images Publishing, 2002)

Pop Architecture, Frances Anderton (Images Publishing, 1998)

ONLINE

Curbed LA, October 11, 2006 – LA Curbed Interviews: Stephen Kanner
www.la.curbed.com

Retail Design Diva, June 21, 2006, Inspiring Spaces – Kanner Studio
retaildesigndiva.blogs.com

Architectural Record, January 2006, Building Types Study: Multifamily Housing – Bentley-Massachusetts Apartments
archrecord.construction.com

Architectural Record, December 2005, House of the Month – Malibu 3
archrecord.construction.com

Architectural Record, May 2002, House of the Month – 511 House
archrecord.construction.com

Architectural Record, 2002, Project Portfolio – Unbuilt Houses – Sagaponac Lot 30
archrecord.construction.com

Architectural Record, 2002, Project Portfolio – Unbuilt Houses – Greer House
archrecord.construction.com

Bentley-Massachusetts
  Size: 12,000 sf
  Budget: $3 million
  Status: Completed 2004
  Owner: Woodcliff Corp.

United Oil Gasoline Station
  Size: 20,600 sf
  Budget: $4 million
  Status: To be completed early 2007
  Owner: Jeff Appel

511 House
  Size: 3,500 sf
  Budget: $850,000
  Status: Completed 2001
  Owner: Stephen Kanner, FAIA

Park Tower
  Size: 800,000 sf
  Budget: Withheld
  Status: Schematic design phase
  Owner: Withheld

Malibu 3
  Size: 4,200 sf
  Budget: $1.5 million
  Status: Completed 2004
  Owner: Richard Feinstein

Ross Snyder Gymnasium
  Size: 12,000 sf
  Budget: $2 million
  Status: Completed 2002
  Owner: City of Los Angeles

Canyon View
  Size: 700 sf
  Budget: $300,000
  Status: Completed 2004
  Owner: Leonard and Joan Beerman

PUMA
  Size: Varies by store
  Budget: Withheld
  Status: Completed between 1999 and 2006
  Owner: PUMA AG

Sagaponac Lot 30
  Size: 3,800 sf
  Budget: $1.5 million
  Status: To be completed 2007
  Owner: The Brown Companies

Metro Hollywood
  Size: 60,000 sf
  Budget: $9.5 million
  Status: Completed 2003
  Owner: McCormack Baron Salazar Inc.

Malibu 5
  Size: 3,300 sf
  Budget: $1.3 million
  Status: Completed June 2006
  Owner: Georgia Goldfarb and Walter Zelman

National Vegetation Classification:
Field guide to mires and heaths

T. Elkington, N. Dayton, D.L. Jackson and I.M. Strachan

Joint Nature Conservation Committee
Monkstone House
City Road
Peterborough
PE1 1JY
UK

ISBN 1 86107 526 X

© JNCC 2001